THE VIKINGS

by Robert Nicholson and Claire Watts

Editorial Consultant: Gareth Binns, Education Officer,
York Archaeological Trust & Council for
British Archaeology

SCHOLASTIC INC.
New York Toronto London Auckland Sydney

ISBN 0-590-46120-6

Copyright © 1991 by Two-Can Publishing Ltd. Text copyright © 1991 by Robert Nicholson. All rights reserved. Published by Scholastic Inc., 730 Broadway, New York, NY 10003, by arrangement with Two-Can Publishing Ltd.

12 11 10 9 8 7 6 5 4 3 2 1   2 3 4 5 6 7/9

Printed in the U.S.A.   08

First Scholastic printing, September 1992

Photographic credits:
Werner Forman: p. 3, p. 6, p. 7, p. 8, p. 9, p. 10, p. 11, p. 12, p. 13, p. 16, p. 17, p. 20 (top) p. 21, p. 23, p. 30 (top), p. 32 (bottom); Toby Maudsley: p. 20 (craft) p. 22; Ronald Sheridan: p. 30 (middle); York Archaeological Trust: p. 19, p. 24

Illustration credits:
Kevin Maddison: p. 9, p. 11, pp. 12-13, p. 14, p. 17, pp. 18-19, pp. 22-23, p. 24
Maxine Hamil cover: pp. 25-29

Contents

The Viking World   **4**

Viking Lands   **6**

Pirates or Traders?   **8**

Longships   **10**

Heroes   **12**

Sagas and Runes   **14**

The Viking Gods   **16**

At Home   **18**

Crafts   **20**

Food   **22**

Clothes   **24**

Thor Visits the Land of the Giants   **25**

How We Know   **30**

Glossary   **31**

Index   **32**

All words marked in **bold** can be found in the glossary.

▼ Eric the Red founded a settlement in Greenland.

▲ The Vikings were the first Europeans to reach America.

Lindisfarne was an island whose wealthy, unprotected monastery was an easy target for the Vikings.

"on 8 june the ravages of heathen men miserably destroyed god's church on lindisfarne with plunder and slaughter…"

(ANGLO-SAXON CHRONICLE, 793)

The Viking World

The first glimpse many European people had of the Vikings was when the fierce dragon-heads of the Viking longships appeared off their coasts. No one was prepared for the invading warriors and few countries could resist the Vikings. From the first attacks in 793, Viking raids were a frequent occurrence all over north-western Europe for the next 200 years.

Key

Key

Discovery routes

Attack routes

Trade routes

◀ Vikings settled in Iceland in the ninth century.

▼ The Vikings who settled in this area were called Rus. The name Russia comes from this word.

▲ The province of Normandy was given to a Viking duke called Rollo by the French king to try to stop him attacking the French coast.

▲ Constantinople was the main city of the powerful **Byzantine** empire. The Vikings traded there.

Viking Lands

The Vikings came from the countries which are now called Sweden, Norway and Denmark. These lands are cold and bleak, with deep rivers, rocky coasts and mountains. There was not enough good farm land to produce sufficient food for all the Vikings, even though they also fished and hunted wild animals.

Many Vikings chose to leave their homes rather than try to farm the meagre land. They set out to seek riches using their skills as seamen and warriors.

Viking lands were divided into several different kingdoms. The richest and most powerful men became leaders and were called kings and dukes. These leaders would sometimes call all the **free men** to a meeting known as the **Allthing** where they would discuss plans about expeditions to other countries or make decisions about local problems. There were often wars between the different kingdoms, particularly over pieces of good land.

▼ Men gathering for the Allthing.

▼ The narrow, deep-watered fjords of **Scandinavia** form perfect natural harbours.

Pirates or Traders?

Pirates

The Vikings attacked lands around them, particularly Britain and France, stealing food and treasures and carrying people off to become slaves. People who lived in isolated areas on the coast or on islands were terrified of the Vikings' attacks. They were mostly farmers, and were not used to defending themselves and their families. They added to their daily prayers the words "God deliver us from the fury of the **Northmen.**"

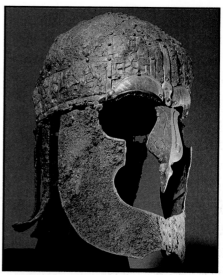

▲ Viking helmets like this one have been found at a number of gravesites in Europe. Soldiers were often buried with all their weapons because the Vikings believed they would need them on the way to heaven.

▼ Rope was wrapped around the hilt of Viking swords to protect the warrior's hand.

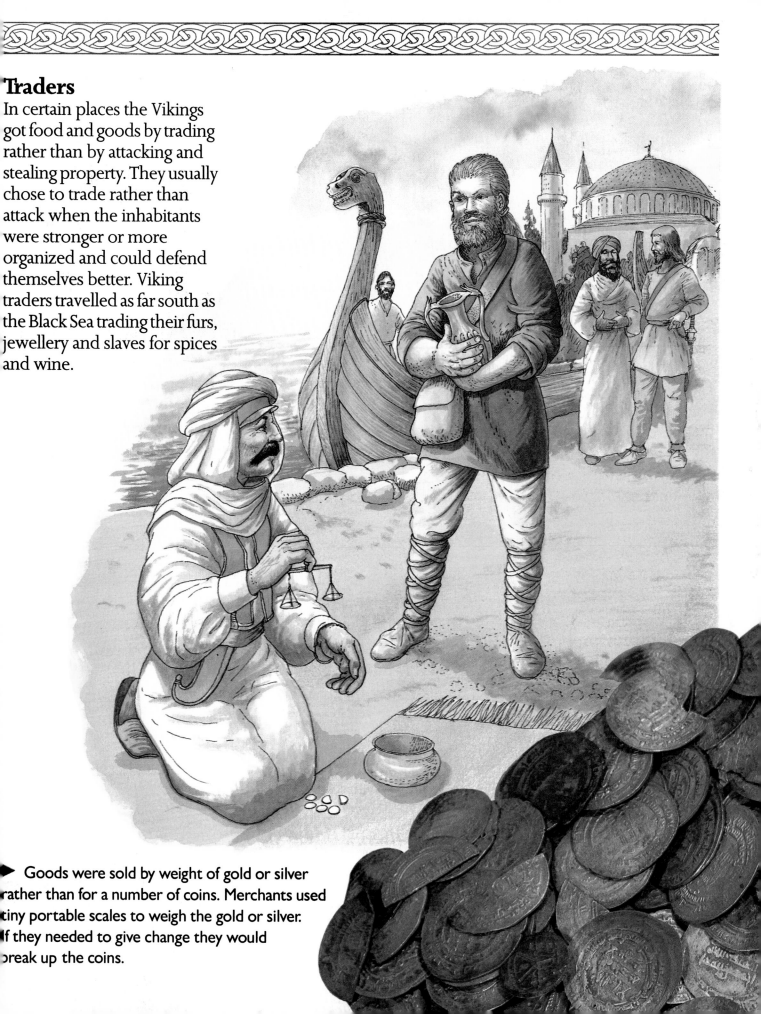

Traders

In certain places the Vikings got food and goods by trading rather than by attacking and stealing property. They usually chose to trade rather than attack when the inhabitants were stronger or more organized and could defend themselves better. Viking traders travelled as far south as the Black Sea trading their furs, jewellery and slaves for spices and wine.

▶ Goods were sold by weight of gold or silver rather than for a number of coins. Merchants used tiny portable scales to weigh the gold or silver. If they needed to give change they would break up the coins.

Longships

The Vikings were superb seamen and used ships for travelling on the lakes, seas and fjords of Scandinavia as well as further afield. The ships were measured by the number of oars they had, the smallest, a **faering**, with 4 and the largest, a **longship**, with about 32. A big longship might be nearly 30 m long and would travel at up to 32 km per hour under full sail. Ships were so important to the Vikings that their language contained dozens of ways of saying "ship".

The Vikings managed to navigate without any of the modern equipment that is used today. They found their way by watching the stars and sun as well as familiar landmarks like islands and mountains. They also looked out for birds which are found in different places at different times of year, like puffins and fulmars.

▲ Viking ships were among the first to have a **keel** which helped them to cut through the water very fast and made them stable even in rough weather.

▲ Oars were used if the sail was not up, when there was no wind or on inland waters. Each rower sat on a box which held his belongings and a waterproof reindeer-skin sleeping bag.

► The gaps between the oak planks of the ship were made waterproof by filling them with sheep's wool dipped in tar.

◄ The ship used one huge square sail. In bad weather this was lowered over the ship and then fastened down like a tent to protect the men inside. The sail was made of thick, coarse material.

◄ The **prow** of a Viking ship was elaborately carved, usually with the head of a dragon or another animal. The ships had names which reflected the shape of their prows, like "Long Serpent", "Snake of the Sea", and "Horse of the Home of Ice".

Heroes

The Vikings admired bold and fearless men and their heroes were all soldiers, sailors or explorers. The deeds of heroes were told again and again until they became more like myths than real historical fact.

Leif Ericson

Eric the Red's son Leif, who was known as "Lucky", arrived in northern America 500 years before Columbus reached the continent. He landed to the south of Newfoundland in a place which he called Markland. He travelled on south to a place called Vinland, which may have been south of modern New York. The Vikings left America after about two years when they were attacked by Indians.

King Cnut

In 1016 England had suffered 200 years of Viking raids, which had made the country very weak. When King Cnut of Denmark attacked England, the English king had just died and so Cnut took over. The English accepted him because he was a wise ruler and brought peace.

Harald Haardraade

As the fame of the Vikings spread throughout Europe, many kings paid Vikings to work in their armies. The Byzantine Emperor had an elite fighting force of Vikings called the **Varangarian Guard.** Harald Haardraade, or Hard-nose, was a famous member of the Guard, who later became king of Norway. He was the last Viking to land with an army in England.

Sagas and Runes

Viking children did not go to school to learn. Lessons came in the form of long stories, or **sagas**, which told the adventures of the gods or of great Viking heroes. These stories were important ways of teaching history, geography and navigation. Children would also learn while helping their parents around the house and farm.

Storytellers travelled around reciting sagas at feasts and festivals. They were especially sought after on dark, cold winter nights, when everyone sat inside around the fire.

▲ Some buildings were decorated with pictures from famous sagas. The wood carving above shows Sigurd the Dragon-Slayer attacking a dragon.

This stone carving shows one of the tales of Odin. You can see Odin in the centre at the top, handing a sword to an old man.

The Futhark

The Viking alphabet, the **Futhark**, was quite different from ours. The letters, or **runes**, are made up mostly of straight lines. This is because they were usually carved into wood or stone and it is easier to carve straight lines than curves.

These are all the runes of the Futhark. Underneath you can see how all the letters were pronounced. Try writing your name in runes – it's like a secret code!

a b c d e f g h

ij k l m n o p q

r s t u v w x y z

The Viking Gods

The Vikings believed that there were lots of different gods who lived in a place called **Asgard.** Each one was responsible for a different thing, like war, travel or the home. In stories the gods were not perfect. They had very human qualities, and also human weaknesses like jealousy and greed.

If a Viking died fighting it was believed that he went to a hall in Asgard called **Valhalla,** where everybody fought all day and feasted all night.

Some Important Gods

Thor

Freyja

Odin

THOR, the god of thunder, was the most popular god. He was short-tempered and a little stupid, but very good-hearted. He had the qualities that the Vikings thought most important: strength and determination.
ODIN or Woden was the god of war, who rode an eight-legged horse. He often doubted himself and spent too long trying to decide whether to do things or not.

FREY made sure that the sun shone, rain fell and the crops grew. He owned a magic boat which could carry all the gods at once, but folded up in his pocket when not needed.
FREYJA was Frey's sister. She was the goddess of love and war. She could turn herself into a bird by putting on a magic falcon-skin.
LOKI was half god, half fire-spirit. He caused the other gods a lot of trouble.

▲ When Viking warriors died their bodies were often placed in longships, which were buried or set alight and pushed out to sea.

▶ Towards the end of the Viking age the Vikings began to convert to Christianity. This is a mould made in the tenth century for making Christian crosses, but it could also be used for making copies of **Mjollnir**, Thor's hammer.

At Home

The Vikings were not only skilled soldiers, seamen and traders. Most Vikings were farmers and lived with their families, growing and making all the things they needed for their daily lives. Children helped their parents as soon as they were able to. Even very small children had their own jobs around the farm, like feeding the animals or gathering firewood.

Viking women worked on the farm and wove material for clothes and blankets on small looms. When their husbands were away fighting, they took care of the whole farm.

Viking houses were made of timber planks and woven branches, with turf or thatched roofs. Stone was used in places where there was no wood, like Shetland and Iceland. Inside, the houses were not divided into rooms. Areas were separated off by stretching cloth or skins between the pillars which supported the roof.

A typical farm would contain the family house, or more than one house if the family were large. There were also sheds for the animals, a workshop with a furnace for making metal tools, and small huts for slaves.

Garbage!

⬤ Viking homes were not as clean as our houses are. Meat bones and vegetable peelings might be left on the floor all winter and only cleared out in the spring.

⬤ Garbage was buried outside.

⬤ All the Vikings had combs because they had lice in their hair.

Games

Viking children did not spend all their time helping their parents. They had some time to themselves for playing games and carving wooden toys. Girls and boys went skating in winter, using skates made of carved bone. These were strapped to the children's shoes with strips of leather.

When it was too dark and cold to go outside, Viking children may have played a game called **hnefatal**. This was a board game rather like chess but with simple pieces, like checkers.

Crafts

Vikings were very skilled craftsmen, making marvellous objects from stone, wood and metal. Many of the most beautiful objects were not made by specialist artists, but by ordinary people. A farmer might make a brooch using the same furnace he used to make his plough.

As there were no banks, people wore their wealth in the form of jewellery. This was the best way to keep it safe.

Smiths were very highly respected and often became very wealthy. Thor, one of the most important Viking gods, used a smith's hammer as his main weapon.

▲ Some jewellery was made specially for burial with a dead person. This arm-ring was found at a burial site.

Make Some Viking Jewellery

Look at the decoration on the Viking objects in this book. Can you see how all the figures are woven around one another? The Vikings loved to use complicated patterns for decoration.

Try making a bracelet or brooch using Viking designs. Modelling clay that you can bake hard in the oven is good for making jewellery.

◀ Use four balls of clay to make the heads.

▼ Roll out three long strands and braid them together.

This is a mould which was used to make part of a helmet. Once the mould was made, many helmets could be made with this pattern.

▶ This gold pendant was worn around the neck as a magical amulet. Look at the elaborate patterns that cover it.

▶ The symbol of Thor's hammer was used in much Viking jewellery. This hammer head is made in silver but many were much simpler than this.

Food

Finding food was a very important part of a Viking's life. Little of the land was fertile and the winters were very long and harsh, so as well as growing and raising food on their farms, the Vikings hunted and fished for food. They ate rich stews of beef or mutton from their farms, or fish and whale meat. They grew vegetables like cabbage, peas and beans and also ate wild leeks and garlic.

Trestle tables would be set up in the middle of the room for meals, and members of the family would sit on the same wooden benches that they slept on at night. They ate off rectangular wooden platters or from soapstone bowls, using spoons and the knives that were carried on their belts at all times.

The Vikings used drinking horns as well as cups. Because the horns did not have flat bottoms, they had to be passed on around the table until they were empty. A man who could drain a drinking horn at one go was very highly thought of! The usual drink was mead, a sweet beer made from honey.

Food Facts

● When the Vikings had no other grain they would use peas to make bread.
● Salt was made by boiling sea-water.
● The Vikings ate two meals a day: the **day meal** after the early farmwork and the **night meal** at the end of the day.

▼ Cooking was done over an open hearth fire. Meat was roasted on huge spits, and stews were made in big iron cauldrons. Sometimes a **gridiron** made of coiled iron was used. Does it remind you of part of a modern stove? Bread was baked in stone ovens or in the ashes of the fire.

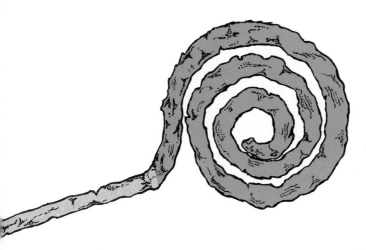

▼ Bowls were made from pottery or soapstone.

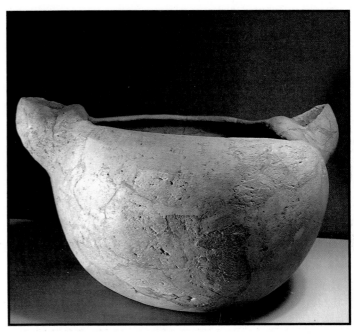

Clothes

Most Viking clothes were made from coarse woollen cloth, although some rich people wore imported silk or linen. In winter people wore furs to keep warm.

Men wore an undershirt and breeches, covered by long woollen trousers and a tunic which reached to the knees. All this was held up with a leather belt. A purse and knife were carried on the belt.

Women wore long wool or linen dresses with a woollen tunic rather like an apron attached with brooches. Hanging from their belts they carried a knife and keys.

▲ Shoes were made from leather or goatskin, laced up with strips of leather.

Thor Visits the Land of the Giants

This story is part of a Viking saga. It is about Thor, the god of thunder, and the journey he set out on to prove his strength. The journey and the trials of strength would have been very familiar to the Vikings.

One summer day, Thor, Loki and their two servants set off to visit Utgard, the land of the giants. After a long journey, they arrived at the gates of Utgard to find them locked. Thor thumped and hammered on the gates, calling out for someone to come and and let them in, but Loki grinned and slipped through the bars, dragging the others after him. They walked into the great hall of Utgard. In the middle of the hall was a long table around which hundreds of giants were seated on benches, eating and drinking and making the most enormous noise. The giants all began to laugh as Thor marched up to the Giant King who was seated on a chair at the far end of the hall.

"Greetings, Giant King," said Thor, politely.

The Giant King sat chewing bones and did not even look at Thor. From time to time he tossed a bone over his shoulder and picked up a new one.

Thor spoke again, a little louder: "Greetings, Gi . . ."

The Giant King interrupted: "So you're the great thunder god Thor, are you? Well, you look like a scrawny little piece of work to me. I suppose you've come to test your strength?"

Thor was furious at the Giant King's rudeness, but it did not seem a very good idea to lose his temper when he was surrounded by giants.

"What skill would you like to challenge us with?" continued the Giant King.

Thor looked around him at the giants.

"I doubt if anyone here can drink as much as I can," Thor replied.

The Giant King signalled to a servant, who brought forward a huge drinking horn.

"This is the horn used by all my followers," he said. "A good drinker can finish it in one draught, and all here can down it in two at the most. Let us see what the great Thor can do!"

Thor took the horn. It was certainly not the largest he had ever drunk from. He raised it to his mouth and began to swallow. He felt sure he could drink it all, but he ran out of breath before the horn was empty. He looked into the horn and found that it was no less full than before. He drank a second time, and again had to stop for breath. This time the horn was no longer brimming full. He took a third draught, gulping down the liquid until he was sure he must empty the horn, but although the level was lower than before, the horn was by no means empty.

"You don't seem to be much of a drinker," said the Giant King. "Why not try your strength? Some of the younger giants like to test themselves by lifting my cat. We don't think this much of a feat, but perhaps you'd like to try?"

Standing beside the Giant King's chair was the most enormous cat Thor had ever seen. He braced himself and then put both arms under the cat and heaved. The cat simply arched its back. Thor heaved again and managed to make the cat lift one paw off the ground before he had to admit defeat.

"As I thought," said the Giant King scornfully. "You may be strong in Asgard and in the realms of men, but your strength is nothing here."

At this Thor grew angry. "I can match any of your men in a fight. Just let anyone here wrestle with me."

There was a roar of laughter from all the giants in the hall.

"Everyone here feels that wrestling with you would be too easy," said the Giant King. "Perhaps you could fight Elli, my foster mother."

A wrinkled old woman hobbled forward leaning on a stick. Thor thought that the Giant King was making fun of him until Elli threw down her stick and took hold of him. He knew at once that his strength would be sorely tested. They struggled and fought, but eventually Elli threw Thor off balance so that he landed on one knee.

"Enough, enough!" shouted the Giant King. "You have shown us that you have no strength as a wrestler either. As you pose no threat to us, you may eat with us and spend the night here in Utgard."

Thor and his companions were very hungry and tired after their long journey. When they had eaten, the tables were pushed back, and they spread their bedding in a space on the floor among the giants.

Thor awoke early, before any of the giants, and roused his companions.

"Come, let's go before the giants wake up," [s]he whispered.

They tiptoed over the sleeping giants and [ou]t of the gates of Utgard. To their surprise, [th]ey found the Giant King already outside [w]aiting for them. He walked with them across [th]e plain for a while.

At last he stopped: "This is where I must [le]ave you. Thor, do not feel too badly about [yo]ur failures last night."

Thor was puzzled. "But I have never before [be]en so soundly beaten," he said.

The Giant King replied: "You were not [co]mpeting in a fair fight. I feared your strength, so I used magic to deceive you. The other end of the horn that you drank from was in the sea. When you reach the shore you will see just how much you have lowered its level. The cat you lifted was really the giant serpent whose body is wrapped around the world. You managed to lift it until its back touched the sky. And as for Elli, it was a wonder you withstood her for so long. You see, Elli is Old Age, which defeats all men in time."

Thor was furious that he had been tricked. He seized his hammer Mjollnir and swung it around his head, but the Giant King and Utgard had vanished, as if they had never been.

29

How We Know

Have you ever wondered how, although the Vikings lived over 1000 years ago, we know so much about their daily lives?

Evidence from the Ground

Certain objects have been found preserved in wet earth or water. Often these are very ordinary objects which were thrown away by the Vikings because they were broken or not needed. Archaeologists piece them together and work out how the Vikings used them.

Some important Vikings were buried in ships full of their possessions. When these ships are discovered, archaeologists can gain a lot of information about the Vikings.

Evidence from Books

Many of the stories told by the Vikings were written down, and so it is quite easy to find out who the important gods were and what various historical figures did. We even know that when Eric the Red discovered Greenland, he gave it that name in spite of its cold iciness because "many would want to go there if it had so promising a name".

Evidence around us

Many place names in Europe were originally Viking names, and so we can tell where the Vikings settled.

The whole of Normandy in France was taken over by the Vikings, and the name means land of the Northmen.

In Britain many place names have the Viking endings "-thorpe" and "-by", like Scunthorpe and Grimsby. Can you find any others on a map?

And what about our days of the week? Did you know that Wednesday was originally Woden's day, and Thursday Thor's day?

Glossary

Allthing
a council of free men which met when problems arose. This was the only form of government the Vikings had.

Asgard
the place where the Vikings believed that their gods lived, and where they would go when they died.

Byzantine
the strongest world power at the time of the Vikings was the Byzantine empire in the east which lasted from the 6th to the 15th century.

Day meal
the first meal of the day, eaten after the early farmwork had been done.

Free men
all the men who were not slaves. Slaves were usually people who had been captured on raids.

Faering
the smallest type of Viking ship, with four oars.

Futhark
the runic alphabet used by the Vikings. The word is taken from the sound of the first six letters.

gridiron
a coiled metal strip which was placed in the fire to heat pots on.

hnefatal
a board game played by the Vikings.

keel
the long timber which forms the lowest part of a ship and helps it to balance.

longship
the long, low ships used by Vikings.

Mjollnir
Thor's hammer. He carried it with him at all times.

night meal
the meal eaten after all the work was done, when it began to grow dark.

Northmen
most of the people the Vikings attacked or traded with knew them as "Northmen". "Viking" was a term they used to describe themselves.

prow
the front end of a ship.

rune
a letter of the Viking alphabet. Runes are made up of straight lines because they were intended to be carved on wood or stone.

saga
storytelling adventure of gods or heroes. Although sagas were usually passed on by word of mouth, some were written down.

Scandinavia
The group of countries which include Denmark, Norway, Sweden and Iceland.

Valhalla
the hall in Asgard where warriors hoped to go when they died. Here they could fight all day and feast all night.

Varangarian Guard
a section of the Byzantine army made up of Vikings. The Varangarian Guard were the Emperor's bodyguard.

Index

Allthing 6
archaeology 30
Asgard 16
attacks 4, 5, 8

Byzantine empire 13

children 14, 18
Christianity 14
clothes 24
Cnut 12
crafts 20, 21

Eric the Red 4, 12, 30
Ericson, Leif 12
expeditions 6, 7

farming 6, 18, 19
food 6, 18, 22, 23
free men 6

Frey 16
Freyja 16
Futhark 15

games 19
gods 16, 17

Haardraade, Harald 13
hero 12, 13, 14
houses 18, 19, 22, 23

jewellery 20, 21, 24

kings 6

Loki 14

Markland 12
Mjollnir 17

navigation 10, 11, 14

Odin 16

runes 14, 15

saga 14, 15
settlements 4, 5
ships 4, 10, 11, 30
slaves 8, 18

Thor 16
trade 5, 9

Valhalla 16
Varangarian Guard 13
Vinland 12

women 18